Beyond "Good Enough"

Getting past "good enough" and onto a better, more productive way of doing business and leading your life.

By

Fred Moore

Cover photos by Craig Fennessy.
www.craigfennessy-photography.com/

For permission requests and information on purchasing more copies of this book, or for information on presentations by Fred Moore, please visit us at:

www.BeyondGoodEnough.com
or
www.MooreFred.com

Dedication:

To my daughter Morgan; Even though at the time of this writing you're only 16 months old you've taught me more than I ever thought.

Now go to bed!

Table of Contents   Page

Sex & Money

I am not going to talk about either of those, but it got you here didn't it? Most people skip over the "introduction" part of the book and I didn't want you to do that, hence the title.

I want to tell you a story. A story of a boy who at the age of six years old, was not only an orphan, but was homeless. A young man, who at the age of nine, was struck by a car and told he would never be able to walk again.

But this young man did go on to not only walk, but to climb to the top of Mount Everest. In the middle of winter, uphill, both ways. Would you believe me if I told you that I am that man?

Well I'm not.

I don't know who that person is. I doubt that person even exists. But we've all heard stories like that, haven't we? Stories of people that overcame tremendous obstacles in their lives and went on to be successful and inspirational people.

Maybe you're like me. And maybe when you hear these stories, you think to yourself, "Wow! That is amazing! If they could overcome these obstacles of theirs, if they can do things with their lives that are just amazing, then surely I can do great things as well."

But then again maybe you're like me. And you hear these stories and you think to yourself, "Wow, I suck. I don't have anything going against me like these people. I don't have any debilitating diseases. I haven't lost any limbs. I don't have anything traumatic that happened in my past. And yet, I haven't done anything with my life. I'm a loser."

It's OK. It's OK to think that way because most of us don't have something like that in our lives to push us, to push us to want to be better. To push us to have to be better than we are. We don't have this traumatic event that has happened to us.

We don't have this challenge, this gauntlet, this thrown at our feet as if to say, "Go ahead, try and be successful. Try to beat these odds. I dare you."

Because if you think about it, even an animal, when they're backed into a corner will turn and fight. If you're pushed hard enough you will, overcome these odds. Or at least die trying, won't you? But most of us don't have that.

We're just stuck in the middle ground. We're at the good enough level in our lives, in our jobs, in our school work. We don't push ourselves to be the best that we can be because we don't have to.

We do things just, "good enough". At our job, we do things just good enough so we don't get fired. An executive once said that it takes an eight-hour day to get five hours of work out of most people. That's because we're just doing things good enough.

In school, we do things just good enough to be average. We don't have to be the A student, do we? We just need to pass. In the US the average grade of a High School student is somewhere between a B and a C. That's average, just good enough to pass.

How about in our relationships? Remember how, when it first started, things were all hot and heavy, and you did everything you could to impress the other person? You did everything you could to make this relationship the best one ever. And as time went on things kind of cooled down a bit, didn't they?

I've heard it said that, a typical couple, in their first year of marriage if they put a quarter into a jar every time they make love, for the first year of their marriage, and then, for the rest of their marriage they take out a dollar from that jar every time they made love, that they will never empty the jar.

I don't know if that's true or not, but I can kind of see how the numbers would work out. Things get cooled off in their marriage, don't they? Life happens. The relationship is good enough. We don't have to try as hard any more do we? Ah, it's good enough, just as long as my wife doesn't yell at me, I'm good.

I was guilty of all these things in my life, in my job, in school, even in my relationships. And I got tired of being just good enough.

When you're just good enough, you get passed over at work. When you're just good enough, you're not noticed at school, you don't excel in your field.

When you're just good enough in your relationships, then people find other people. You thought it was good enough, but for them, it's just not good enough.

My name is Fred Moore, and I have spent my life trying to improve myself, my life, my work, my relationships, everything. I've done this by studying all the Masters out there when it comes to time management, goal setting, motivation, mindset and productivity.

Along the way, I've learned some things. I've learned how to set a goal, how to go past "good enough" and go beyond "good enough".

Hey, what a great title for a book!

Who Is This Guy?

I want to give you some background of who I am and where I've come from.

I grew up in a small little town in Ohio. Not much going on there. And at the ripe, old age of 16, I knew what I wanted to do for a living. I knew that I wanted to be a magician.

That's right, you heard me. I wanted to do magic. I wanted to be the next David Copperfield, the next Doug Henning. Or for you younger folks, I wanted to be the next Chris Angel, or David Blaine.

Here's the thing. When I sat down with my High School guidance counselor, and he asked me, "What do you want to do for your career? What do you want to do for the rest of your life?" I looked him square in the eyes, I said, "I want to be a Magician."

He looked at me and said, "Well………………. Good luck with that." He had no clue what to tell me.

If I wanted to be a plumber, he knew what direction to point me in. If I wanted to be a professor, he knew where to direct me. But nobody had ever told him that they wanted to be a Magician. He had no idea what to tell me.

I totally understand that. I had no idea how to become a Magician. I knew that I would need to learn how to do magic. Now just because you can do magic doesn't mean you can make your living as a Magician.

I had to learn how to be my own producer, my own director, my own seamstress. I had to figure out where the gigs were and how to get them, how to contact people, how to promote myself, how to put together a good promotional video tape.

Now what does all this have to do with you and going beyond good enough? Well I learned how to be self-sufficient. I learned how to be a self-motivator. I learned how to set goals and get them achieved.

See that's the magic formula right there. You can set a goal, but if you don't get that goal, well then it's not really doing you any good, is it?

That's what this book is all about. All about helping you go beyond "good enough. "

As you go through this book you may see some things repeated. Or you may see some things repeated. Or repeated.

It's not that I have A.D.D. or anything it's just that…oh wait! What's that over there?

There are two reasons why some parts are repeated. The first is that what I'm saying is really important for you to get and understand. Sometimes we miss things as we're plowing through a book.

The second reason is that some people like to jump around in a book and only get to the parts that they think are relevant to them. So the important points are repeated just for them.

Thanks for making it this far, let's get to it!

Chapter 1
A Crash Course in Productivity

In order for you to get what you want out of life or your business; you need to know specifically what it is that you want.

Well duh!

Let me explain, a lot of people will set a goal like this; "I want to lose weight.", "I want to be rich." Well what's wrong with that? There's nothing wrong with those goals. It's just that they're not specific; they're not clearly defined goals. They're just arbitrary statements.

They're just, "I wish", "I want to", "I hope". They are not concrete goals. They're just random statements.

It's like New Year's resolutions. December 31st, the ball drops in Times Square and everyone makes resolutions. "This year my resolution is I'm going to lose weight. I'm going to stop smoking. I'm going to get out of debt. I'm going to start my own business."

Then what happens? Usually nothing. Nothing happens until the end of the year when it's December 31st again. And you think back, "Oh yeah, I forgot about that resolution from last year. OK. This year will be different, yeah, yeah that's it." And the vicious cycle starts all over again.

That's why, if you're going to complete a goal and get the results that you want, you need to have a clearly defined, specific, goal.

Define Your Goal

Let's take a couple of these examples. "I want to lose weight." Instead of saying "I want to lose weight." state it specifically. How much weight do you want to lose? Not "I want to lose weight." or "I want to be skinny." but how much weight do you want to lose? How much weight are you going to lose?

Then your goal statement would be like this: "I want to lose 20 pounds." That's a pretty clear goal, pretty specific.

How about a business type goal? Instead of "I want to be rich." it would be "I want to make $5,000.00 more. I want to have $5,000.00 more money in the bank."

Pretty specific, but there's a problem with both of these goals. There's no deadline. There's nothing to push you to try to achieve this goal, is there? There's no deadline looming over the horizon to make you work towards this goal.

Set A Deadline

Maybe you're like me and in school, the night before the big test is when you studied the hardest. The night before that term paper was due was when you maybe started on it, but you know for sure that you had to complete it that night and you pulled an all-nighter.

Because you had a deadline, it had to be done by this time. So set a deadline for your goal. You want to lose 20 pounds? When do you want to lose it by? Set a specific day that you're going to have those 20 pounds off; two months from now, six months from now, whatever.

Just make sure it's a specific date. Don't state it as, "In two months I'm going to lose weight." No, put down a specific date. Because if you look back on this goal a week later, it says "In two months, I'm going to lose 20 pounds."

Well, you still have two months, don't you? But no, if you have a specific date, you know when you have to lose that weight.

With the money goal, the same thing, make it specific: "By the end of this month..." "By the 31st of January, I want to make $5,000.00 more." Now your goal is specific and it has a deadline.

But when you're setting this deadline make sure it's a realistic deadline. Don't set yourself up for failure by setting a deadline that is not achievable.

Now I want you to go for the gold, as it were, or in this case goal; go for the goal. See what I did there? But I want to make sure that you're not setting yourself up for failure.

You're thinking "Why would you do this?" Well, people like to be able to justify to themselves that they tried to do something and it didn't work, so now they don't have to try it again, do they?

For instance: somebody might set a weight loss goal of, "I want to lose 20 pounds by next week." It's not a very realistic goal. Is it possible? I don't think so.

They only way I can think of to lose 20 pounds by next week would be to lose a limb or go gambling in the UK. Think about it, 20 pounds, UK, gambling, it's money. I'll wait for it, go ahead.

It's not a very realistic goal, is it? Twenty pounds by next week, not very realistic.

Make It Realistic

How do you figure out when would be a good deadline? Well, it's a little thing called math. Run away kids, we're doing math!

Let's say that your goal is, "One month from now, I want to lose 20 pounds." That's about four weeks, on average. So do the math; 20 pounds divided by four weeks, that's five pounds a week. Five pounds a week might be possible, but it probably wouldn't be very healthy.

You could possibly do it but you'd jeopardize your health in the process, in my opinion; I'm not a doctor, I'm not advising you one way or the other, I just don't think it's a very realistic deadline.

So, increase the deadline. Let's make it two months, let's make it eight weeks, that's two and a half pounds a week. Two and a half pounds a week is doable. You could probably lose two and a half pounds a week if you just stop drinking soda and start walking three times a week.

Again, I'm not a doctor or trainer. That may not work for anyone. Please enjoy this disclaimer now; your mileage may vary, void where prohibited.

But at least that goal is more concrete. That deadline is achievable, and if it seems like it's just a little too much for you, bump it up.

Instead of eight weeks, make it ten weeks. That's two pounds a week. But if you really, really want to set yourself up for success instead of setting yourself up for failure, double that deadline. Twenty weeks, twenty pounds; that's one pound a week. If you can't lose one pound a week, then obviously you're not doing anything right. Chances are, you're probably not doing anything about this goal.

How about the money goal? Let's say you want to make $5,000.00 more. Well what's your deadline? By the end of the month, that's your deadline. In one month's time $5,000.00. Is that achievable? Is that doable?

Let's think about it. Let's say you own a business and you're open seven days a week, on average 30 days in the month, $5,000.00 divided by 30, is around $167.00 a day. So that means, in your business, you need to bring in an extra $167.00 in revenue every single day, to achieve this goal of $5,000.00 in that month.

Look at your business; is that a realistic goal? Can you bring in that much money in one day, and can you do it consistently? If you want to break it down to the hour, you can do that. Let's say you're open ten hours in the day, that's $16.70 every hour that you need to ring up in that register.

If you look at that and you think, "that's doable", then you have a realistic deadline. If it's not doable, either decrease the amount of money, or increase the time.

Do the math and make things work right. Get this deadline so it's very specific and narrowed down and it's achievable.

Why would somebody set up an unrealistic deadline? They want to be able to justify to themselves, "Well look I tried to do it and it didn't work, so now I'm just not going to try at all. I tried it, didn't work, OK. I can go back to the way things were, I was unhappy and fat, and didn't have any money. But at least now I don't have to work towards my goal."

Now you have a clearly defined goal, with a specific deadline. Now you need to state it as if it's already happened. State it as if it's a foregone conclusion.

State It Properly

Don't state it as "I want" or "I wish."

In other words, don't state it like "I want to lose 20 pounds in eight weeks." or "I wish I would make $5,000.00 more this month."

My grandma used to say "Wish in one hand and spit in the other, see which one fills up first." OK, she didn't say spit, but you get the idea.

Instead of saying, "I want..." or "I wish..." state it like this, "As of July 31st I <u>have</u> lost 20 pounds.", "As of January 1st I <u>have</u> made $5,000.00 more." You see the difference there?

You're stating it as if it's already happened. And when you do this it triggers a different part of your brain. Instead of thinking,

"Oh I want..." or "I wish I had this." it starts thinking "I have done this. Well how did I get it done?

If it's already happened, I've done it, which means it's possible. It's a possibility, it can be done. How am I going to do it?" Seems very basic, seems kind of simplistic, I know, but trust me, this stuff works.

Make It Personal

You want to add a little meaning behind this goal. Make it personal. So instead of, "By July 31st I have lost 20 pounds." state it like this, "As of July 31st, I have lost 20 pounds of ugly fat and I look good." You see now there's some meaning behind this goal. It's 20 pounds of ugly fat.

Instead of just 20 pounds it's ugly fat, it's ugly and it's fat, it's something that you don't want. And you look good. There is your reward, that's your outcome for this goal.

If you don't know what the outcome for your goal is, it's not going to have as much meaning for you. That's your reward, that's the bonus, that's what you're going to get after all this blood, sweat, and tears. You're going to look good because you've lost 20 pounds of ugly fat.

How about the money goal? Instead of, "As of January 1st, I have made $5,000.00 more." put a little meaning behind it, put a little meat behind it. "As of January 1st, I've $5,000.00 more and now I'm going to take a trip to Hawaii and treat myself to a Hawaiian Luau."

See, there's a reward built in. Now, I wouldn't advise doing that every single month, otherwise you are not going to have that $5,000.00, are you? It doesn't have to be a Hawaiian trip, you get the idea, use your imagination.

Make your goal statement personal. Make it real for yourself.

There is your clearly defined, specific goal, with a deadline and stated as if it's already happened, with a little personality behind it.

That is the first step in our G.A.M.E. plan for success. What's a G.A.M.E. plan you ask? I'm glad you asked that! It's an acronym. It stands for;

Goal
Action
Motivation
Evaluation

Goal is obviously the first step in the plan. You have to have a clearly defined goal to get what you want. We know that and it's in this specific order for a reason.

Just like when you're baking a cake. You're not going to put flour in the oven and turn it to 365 degrees and let it bake for 20 minutes before you add egg and milk and everything else in it.

If you get the order of the recipe all mixed up, you're not going to get the cake. You're not going to get the result that you want. That's why I came up with the G.A.M.E. plan.

Before we move onto the next step in our G.A.M.E. plan, I've included some of my favorite quotes about goals, enjoy!

Set your goals high, and don't stop till you get there.

-Bo Jackson

What you get by achieving your goals is not as important as what you become by achieving your goals.

-Henry David Thoreau

Learn from the past, set vivid, detailed goals for the future, and live in the only moment of time over which you have any control: now.

-Denis Waitley

Discipline is the bridge between goals and accomplishment.

-Jim Rohn

Setting goals is the first step in turning the invisible into the visible.

-Tony Robbins

I've worked too hard and too long to let anything stand in the way of my goals. I will not let my teammates down and I will not let myself down.

-Mia Hamm

The game has its ups and downs, but you can never lose focus of your individual goals and you can't let yourself be beat because of lack of effort.

-Michael Jordan

How To Set A Goal

1. Clearly define your goal.
    Exactly what is it that you want?
    Be as precise as you can.

2. Set a realistic deadline for this goal.
    Make sure you're not setting yourself
    up for failure and that you can and
    will complete this goal.

3. State the goal as if it's already happened.
    Don't use the words "I want" or "I
    wish" instead state it as "I have".

4. Make it personal.
    Put some meaning behind your
    goal and make it count.

Chapter 2
Let's take some action.

Action is the next step in the G.A.M.E. plan. You have a clearly defined goal. Now, it's time to start doing something about your goal.

What a novel idea, huh? I mentioned before about New Year's resolutions, and that's another reason why they usually don't work. People make the resolution, it's a great idea, it's obviously something that they want to do. Otherwise why would you say it, right?

But they don't do anything about it. Or, if they do, it's not a specific action step that they're taking, it's just something random. They want to stop smoking, so what do they do? They stop smoking. They just quit.

Think about it, they've been smoking a long time, they didn't just start suddenly, and then they were addicted to it. It started slowly.

They want to lose weight, what do they do? Join a gym. January is the best month for gym memberships. Gyms run specials, they advertise, and more people sign up in the month of January than in any other month throughout the year. Because of New Year's resolutions. "I want to lose weight, I will join a gym."

So they go down, they sign the paperwork, and they join a gym. And what do they do? Maybe they go to the gym. Maybe they exercise, they work out and things are going great... for a little while.

Then things sort of taper off. New Year's is over, it's January, it's a new year, things happen, Valentine's Day, "Oh look, let's go out and celebrate. Look, it's March. Hey, let's go out and celebrate Saint Patrick's Day," they forget about the gym and they stop taking action.

They had the right idea at the beginning but they weren't specific with what actions they were going to be taking. You can see there's a theme to this, isn't there.

I'm very big on being specific with everything. Your goal is specific, so your action steps should be specific as well.

When you have your goal statement, sit down and figure out "What am I going to do to make this goal happen? What am I going to do to create this reality? What action steps am I going to take, right now?" Figure out what it is you need to do to make this goal happen, and make it specific.

Instead of, "I'm going to join a gym," make it specific. What are you going to do? "Join the gym, and I'm going to start a weight training program. I'm going to take Zumba classes, I'm going to take yoga, I'm going to work on my cardiovascular. I'm going to hire a trainer. I'm going to start jogging; I'm going to start swimming."

Make It Specific

Make it specific. What exactly are you going to do?

For the money goal, what action steps are you going to take to make more money? If you want to increase your sales, what are you going to do? Who are you going to talk to? Do you need to hire someone else? Do you need to fire somebody else?

Exactly what are you going to do to make this goal happen? Taking action is one of the biggest things that people don't do. It's one of the most important steps in the G.A.M.E. plan, doing something, taking action towards your goal.

True Story

My background is in entertainment, in case you didn't get that before, and I was doing a tour with a big company. We toured for two years. We toured in Europe for one year, and then in South America the next year.

I'd been contracted for the U.S. tour for nine months. Nine months, I was going to be on tour in the U.S. with this show, which was great, because that meant I didn't have to look for any other work. I had a nine-month contract.

Granted, this contracted did have a six week out clause in it. Past six weeks, the contract was good. In that six week period, if things didn't work out between us, they could let me go, or I could leave. No harm, no foul.

About two weeks into this contract I was called into a production meeting, and in walks the head of HR. Never a good sign, right?

We chit-chatted for a little bit, and then he informed me that they were releasing me from my contract. I love how they said it. "We're releasing you from your contract." I just got fired. That's it. Plain and simple.

You're out of here. No nine month contract, no work for the next nine months for you, nothing.

I have to tell you, I was not a happy camper. Not a happy camper at all. I'd been turning work down because I thought I had the next nine months booked up. But now suddenly I didn't.

What did I do? Well, I did take a moment or two to express my unhappiness to myself. I kept my calm in the meeting of course, I said "I totally understand," and I asked them why, and if there's anything I can do, no, okay, great. Then I spent about an hour or so being a little bit miserable.

But I knew that wasn't going to do me any good, so what did I do? Well, if you don't know, then look at the title of this chapter. I took some action. I took some action towards my goal, because my goal now was to find some work.

I had no work at all, so I needed to find something, I needed to have some money rolling in, soon. That was my deadline, my deadline was yesterday. And I had some good motivation, because I wasn't going to be able to eat, I wasn't going to be able to pay the mortgage, I wasn't going to be able to feed my family. I needed to find work, and I needed to find it now.

So I took action. Not just action, I took what Tony Robbins calls massive action. I did anything and everything I could think of to find work. I got on the phone, I called my agent, I called other agents, I called agents who never even heard of me, and introduced myself to them. I called my friends, I told them what had happened, let them know I was going to be in town, so if anything came up, let me know.

I went back to old contacts, people I'd worked for years before, and contacted them to see if they could use my services again. I started looking in places I never looked for work before. But now, it was an option, because it was there.

I got the ball rolling, because I took action. I took action towards my goal. I took action towards this problem that I had, and I solved this problem, because I got some work rolling in. It took me a couple of weeks, but I started getting contracts, I started getting bookings, I got three weeks in Japan, I got booked six weeks on a cruise ship. I got things rolling by taking action and lots of it!

In that nine month period when I would have been working for this company, instead I was working for myself and doing what I loved. I worked about half the time and made just a little bit more money than I would have made if I'd stayed with this company, working for them.

I took action towards my goal. I solved my problem by taking action. Taking action can help you solve your problems, because if you sit there and have a problem, worrying about it, and moaning about it, it's probably not going to do you a whole lot of good.

But by taking action towards this problem, it will help you solve this problem. It will help this problem to disappear, as it were.

Action Cures Fear

Taking action can also help you conquer fear. Have you ever been afraid to go to the dentist? Maybe you're not afraid to go to the dentist, but you probably don't like to go to the dentist. And if you do like to go to the dentist, either you're a masochist, or you have really good teeth, and you never have any problems or pain while you're at the dentist. But a lot of people don't like to go to the dentist, and I'm one of them. Never looked forward to going to the dentist.

But what happens after you go to the dentist? This fear you've had, this hesitation, this trepidation of going to the dentist, is now gone. Because, it's over now, isn't it? You took action, and now this fear is gone. Action cures fear.

If you're afraid of picking up that phone and asking that person out, once you do it, the fear is gone. Now, the result you get doesn't matter, whether you got a yes or a no, but that fear that you had, the hesitation is now gone.

If you've ever had to make a sales call, a cold call, you can understand that cold clammy feeling that comes over you when you're picking up the phone and dialing that person that has never heard of you, and probably doesn't want to hear from you. But you have to make the call, don't you? And once you make the call, it's over. It's done. Action cures fear.

What To Do

But, what actions should you take? What are you going to do to make this problem disappear, what are you going to do to make your goals a reality? Here's a simple technique that I use to brainstorm ideas of actions that I can take.

I make a 50-ways list. 50 ways. 50 ways to lose weight, 50 ways to make more money, 50 ways to start my own business. I make a list. I start writing down 50 ways on how I want to make this goal happen.

For instance, 50 ways to lose weight, so, you'd start writing things down, like, "I'm going to join a gym, I'm going to stop eating sugar, I'm going to stop drinking soda, I'm going to go for a walk every day." Now, why 50 ways?
Because if you just limit yourself to 20 ways, you could probably come up with 20 ways on how to do just about anything. 20 ways to lose weight, you could come up with. 20 ways to make more money, you could come up with 20 ways.

But when you push yourself to have to come up with 50 ways, 50 ways on how to do this goal of yours, then you start to get a little creative. You're going to start to think outside of the box, you're going to start to think of ways that you wouldn't have thought of if you just limited yourself to 20 ways.

Plus, you're going to make these action steps more specific. Instead of just, "I'm going to join a gym," it's going to be what, specifically, are you going to do to lose that weight, "I am going to start lifting weights, I am going to jog around the lake every morning for 20 minutes."

You're going to get very specific with your action steps, because you need to come up with 50 of them. You need to come up with 50 ways on how to do whatever it is that you want to do.

Don't stop until you get at least 50. Here's a cool thing you can do, is don't number them. Just start writing down the ideas; you're brainstorming at this point. You're just throwing ideas out there. Throwing ideas, you can see if they stick later on. But just start writing, write, write, write, keep on writing until your hand cramps, or your fingers cramp up from typing. Just keep on writing until you can't think of any more.

Then total up, see if you've got 50. If you don't, then put those to the side. Give it some time, let your brain recharge, and then come back to it later on. Not too long, couple of hours, maybe even a day. But come back to it, and get at least 50 ways.

If you did get 50 ways the first time, it doesn't matter. Put it aside, come back to it again. You'll probably come up with some more ideas.

The more ideas you have, the better chances of your success, because now you have more action steps to pull from. You can figure out which one of these is going to work.

That's what the next step is, taking a look at this list of yours, going through it, and picking out the top ten ways, the top ten ideas that you think are going to get you the best results.

Because if you just look at this list of 50 things that you need to do, it's going to overwhelm you. "That's too much stuff to do, I can't do it, I won't even start." Pick out the top ten ways, the top ten ways that you can lose weight, the top ten ways you can make more money, and start doing those.

In fact, of those ten, pick one that you can do right away, something that you can do at that exact moment, because you're going to get momentum going.

You're going to take some action, which is going to lead to you to taking some more action, which will take you to the next step, and the next step.

Here comes the science part, kids. You know what they say. An object in motion tends to stay in motion. If you don't know what you need to do, look at your list. You have a list of 50 ways on how to do exactly what you want to do.

Now, not all of these ideas are going to be great ideas. Some of them may be crazy ideas. Some of them probably won't work at all. But it doesn't matter. You've got your creative juices flowing. You've thought of some ideas, you've got the ball rolling, because you're taking action towards this goal of yours. You're not just sitting around and thinking about it, and "I wish, I hope this would happen, I don't know if it's going to or not." No. You're taking action!

Before we move onto the next step in the G.A.M.E. plan please enjoy these quotes on taking action.

When it is obvious that the goals cannot be reached, don't adjust the goals, adjust the action steps.   -Confucius

Love begins at home, and it is not how much we do... but how much love we put in that action.   -Mother Teresa

Do you want to know who you are? Don't ask. Act! Action will delineate and define you.
                    -Thomas Jefferson

Action speaks louder than words but not nearly as often.   -Mark Twain

I never worry about action, but only inaction.
                    -Winston Churchill

Action expresses priorities.
                    -Mahatma Gandhi

Action is the foundational key to all success.
                    -Pablo Picasso

Take Some Action

1. Decide your actions.

   Clearly define what steps you're going to take to make your goal happen.

2. If you fear an action do it now!

   The sooner you take that action, the sooner it will be over and you can move onto other actions.

3. Make a 50 Ways list.

   If you're not sure what to do to make your goal a reality, make a list of at least 50 ways you can do to make your goal happen.

Chapter 3
Are You Motivated?

Motivation. I'm not talking about the kind of motivation where it's like "You can do it if you think positive thoughts. Only focus on rainbows and unicorns." Not that kind of motivation. I'm talking about the kind of motivation that is going to keep you on track with this goal of yours.

Why would you need motivation? After all, it's your goal, isn't it? Well, think about it. This is probably a goal you've been wanting for a while. You've been at it for a while. You've tried it before and it hasn't worked. So, obviously, you need something to motivate you to complete this goal of yours.

Maybe this goal isn't yours. Maybe it's somebody else's goal. Maybe it's a deadline, a goal that you've been given by your boss or your higher-ups or your spouse or somebody else in the world.

So, it's not really your goal. You need to find something that is going to motivate you to want to complete this goal. It's not your idea.

It's probably not your favorite thing to do in the world. You need to find yourself something to keep you motivated.

Why are you going to get this goal completed? Now, obviously, if this was a goal that was handed to you from your boss the big motivation behind that would be "You're going to get fired."

But maybe the motivation is the consequences if you don't get this goal completed. If it's a goal that your spouse has given you and you don't take out the garbage, well guess what? You're going to be in trouble.

Sometimes, we need a little bit more motivation to complete our goals. Because doing the things that we need to do to get this goal done are going to be painful. We're going to have to give up something. We're not going to have that pleasure of whatever it is that we're giving up. Let me give an example.

Let's say it's a weight-loss goal. You want to lose some weight. Well, it's going to be painful to lose this weight. Because you're going to have to exercise, you're going to have to work. You're going to have to push yourself and muscles are going to be sore. You're going to be sweaty, you're going to be smelly and you have to make some sort of an effort.

Plus, you're going to miss out on the pleasure that you have from eating all that good stuff. Eating all the sweets. Eating all the really yummy food out there. And denying yourself that is going to cause you pain.

Psychologically, we are programmed to do more to avoid pain than to gain pleasure. We will do more to avoid all that bad stuff, all the feeling of working and denying yourself the sweets.

We'll do more to avoid that than we will to gain the pleasure of a healthy lifestyle. Of, perhaps, living another 20 years and not dying early.

It sounds insane, doesn't it? Why would you not want to have those things? Because those things are not immediately apparent to us when we're in the middle of this goal.

We live in a society that is about instant gratification, we want it right now! If we can't see what our goal is, if we're not going to have it right now, then it's really difficult for us to grasp onto it. To really make it ours and to keep ourselves motivated to get this goal.

A weight-loss goal is not going to happen overnight. So, you have to keep yourself motivated. If it's a money-type goal, you want to save more money, you want to make more money. Again, it's not an instant thing.

Unless you go ahead and sell off the diamond that you've been hiding in your closet for $50,000, you're probably not going to come out with instant cash right away. It's going to be something that's going to happen in the future. So, you need to keep yourself motivated towards this goal.

I'll tell you a few ways that I like to keep myself motivated.

Goal Wall

This is a wall I have in my office. It can be anywhere you want. It can be on your computer desktop.

It can be on your Smartphone, on the fridge, on the mirror in your bathroom. But it's very important that this wall is someplace that you go every day, someplace that you're going to see it every single day.

That's why I keep mine in my office. I'm always in my office. Ask my wife, she'll tell you.

On this goal wall, I have, guess what? My goals. You are so smart. I have my goals printed out and stuck up on my wall. I have my clearly-defined goal. Remember we talked about that in the first of the game plan, my goal, right?

My clearly-defined goal with a specific deadline and it's stated as if it's already happened.

Below that, I'll list a few of the top action steps that I'm going to take to make this goal happen.

I print it out and I stick it up on my goal wall. Now, at any given time, I'm going to have six or seven different goals up there. It depends. Your mileage may vary, as it were. Do whatever works for you.

But now, I have a daily reminder of my goals. It's up there in front of me, so I can see it every single day. This is what I'm going to get. There's the date I'm going to get it and those are the steps I need to take to make it all happen. It's a daily reminder of the goals that I have and what I am going to get accomplished.

Once I've completed a goal, I don't just take it down and throw it away, no. I take a big, black marker and I put a check mark right across. Not an "X," but a check mark. Check is completed, "X" means "No." So, it's a check mark. I've completed this goal.

I take it down and I put it down at the bottom. Right at the bottom of the goal wall. And I just sort of line them up. Sort of like the old World War II pilots would have the little "Kill" stickers on the side of their airplanes, the little decals, to show them how many planes they've shot down.

Well, this is your trophy wall because now at the bottom, you have whole lists there. A whole list of the goals you have accomplished and things that you've gotten done.

So, anytime you're looking at your goal wall and you think to yourself "Maybe I can't do that. Maybe it's too much." All you have to do is look down and you can see all the goals that you've already completed.

Now, I said you can use it on your wall. You can use it as your wallpaper on your computer screen. On your Smartphone, that can be the wallpaper. Every time you turn it on, boom, that's what you see. You see your goals stated there. What you want to get and when you're going to make it happen.

Tell A Friend

Another way to motivate yourself is to tell a really good friend about this goal you have. Make a public declaration of what it is that you're going to do, when you're going to do it and how you're going to make it happen.

Tell your friend about your goal and help them to motivate you. Help them to encourage you with this goal of yours. Hopefully, it's a good friend that they'll be able to call you on things that maybe, you shouldn't be doing.

For instance, if it's a weight-loss goal and maybe the one sitting there at lunch going "Are you going to have dessert? I thought you were going to lose weight."

Now, you may resent them at the time, but later on, you'll think to yourself "You know, they're right. They're a really good friend. I'm glad I shared this goal of mine with them."

Maybe this friend has a similar goal. Maybe you can partner up. You can be goal buddies. You can hold each other accountable for this goal. Set the same sort of goal.

Again, if it's a weight-loss goal, you can be workout buddies. If it's a financial goal, you can compete to see who can save more money that week or that month or that year. Partner up with a friend of yours. Tell a good friend about your goal and let them motivate you.

Another way to keep yourself motivated is to tell a not-so-good friend about your goal. What? Stick with me, here.

We all know the type of person that relishes reminding all of us of our failures. They love to bring it up in your face like "Oh, remember when you didn't get that done"? Or if you failed at something, they want to be right there when it happens. So, they could go "Uh, huh. I knew you couldn't do it. I just knew you'd fail."

That type of person that just loves to get under your skin. And prove to you that you are a failure.

If you don't know a person like this, there's a good chance it's you. That's all I'm saying here. I'm not judging people, I'm just saying.

Why would you want to tell a person like this about this goal that you have? To motivate yourself because you know if you tell this person "All right, look. By this date, I'm going to drop 20 pounds. By this date, I'm going to have an extra $5,000 in my bank account. By this date, I'm going to have this many sales with this company."

You know for a fact that that person will come around on that exact date, probably the first thing in the morning and come up to you and go "Hey, how's that little goal of yours coming up? Weren't you supposed to be done with it now"?

If you know that person is going to be coming around, you'll probably be pretty highly motivated. Maybe you'll call in sick that day, so you can avoid them and hope they'll forget about it.

But you won't have to. Because you have a G.A.M.E. plan, don't you? You've motivated yourself, you're using this person to help you complete your goal.

You can sit there and just wait for them to show up at your door and ask you "So, did you get it done"? And you look them straight in the eyes and go "Not only did I get it done, but I got it done before my deadline and I got more done than I wanted to do."

Basically, in your face!

Quotes

Another great way that I like to keep myself motivated is to put up a motivational quote where I can see them all the time. Now, stick with me here. I know it kind of sounds New Age-y and "Surround yourself with the positive." But guess what? That stuff works. That's why we've all heard it time and time again.

Remember back in the '80s, early '90s, they had those motivational posters everywhere? "Innovation," "Perseverance," "Success." Well, those were great. I loved those. I had a bunch of those. I had the catalog, that's how much I loved them. You could probably tell I loved this kind of stuff.

Well, I continued on because I don't have those posters anymore. But what I do have are lots and lots of books with positive motivational quotes.

I love to just open up the book whenever I'm having some leisure time and sitting down and want to read something. I think you get the idea of where I do a lot of my reading.

I love to pull out one of these books with positive and motivational quotes before I get ready to do a presentation or a show. I'll sit down and get my brain in the frame of mind, in a positive frame of mind. I don't want to be performing on stage and presenting with negative thoughts in my head. I want to be in a positive mode.

My job is to help people change their lives. So, I need to be in that positive mode. And that's why I like to use these positive motivational quotes.

I've got eBooks on my Smartphone that I'll read through a couple of quotes before I go onstage. And my favorite ones I like to print out and put on my wall. Kind of like those posters, but smaller versions.

I put them on my wall, put them on my bathroom mirror, I put them anywhere and everywhere I can. That way, I'm constantly surrounding myself with this good, positive motivation.

Record Your Goals

Another way that you can keep yourself motivated is to record your goals, either a video recording or an audio recording. Put it on to a CD or an MP3; hook it up to a Bluetooth to your car or phone, whatever you have to do. Then first thing in the morning when you start that car and head to work, go ahead and play that recording.

Play the recording of the goals that you've set for that month, for that week, for that year. It'll be a daily reminder of the goals you've set and the action-steps you're going to take. And the deadline you've set for yourself.

It's a great way to keep this goal of yours top of mind. And then do the same thing at the end of the night before you go to bed, while you're brushing your teeth, fixing your hair or taking off your makeup. Whatever you're doing to get ready for bed go ahead and play this recording again.

It's the last thing your mind will hear before it goes to bed. And your subconscious brain will go to work on these goals.

You'll wake up in the morning, you'll probably think of some ideas that you hadn't thought of before. You might even wake up in the middle of the night with a brilliant idea to help you accomplish one of these goals.

Do yourself a favor. When that happens, write it down immediately. Because I can almost guarantee you will forget it by the time you wake up.

You'll think to yourself "Oh, man, I had a great idea. Now, I can't remember it." And then you'll think back, "I should have listened to Fred. That bald guy knows what he's talking about."

Here's a funny little story of motivation. I mentioned before that I used to run those 5K races. And this one particular race was very psychologically daunting because the last part of it was a long stretch of road with the goal not in sight anywhere at all. Well, I had broken that goal down like I mentioned before, into smaller bits. But I also gave myself a little bit of motivation.

This was back in the days when I was young and dumb and single. So, just ahead of me, about 10, 15 feet, was a young lady. She was around my age and from my view, very attractive. Look, I'm a guy. Please, no letters, no e-mails, okay? I'm a guy, I can't help it.

I was thinking to myself "Okay, here's an attractive girl running this same race. We already have something in common. We're both crazy for doing this in the first place, right? After this race is over, I'm going to talk to her. I'm going to talk to her and I don't know if she's single, I don't know anything about her, but that she's ahead of me and she's pretty good-looking from my view."

There's my motivation. I was keeping pace with her, that's my motivation. Sort of the carrot and the stick. I'm going to talk to her after the race.

I kept pace, it kept me going. I knew "All right, this is great. This is great. At the end of the race, I'm going to talk to her; I'm going to talk to her. This is great. Keep going, keep going, keep going."

Well, the story does not end well. You see, my frail male ego got in the way. As we're approaching the finish line I had to try and be cool; to show her what a manly man I was.

So, I'm going to sprint. I'm going to sprint right by her and finish before she does. And she'll see "Look at that energy. Look at that virile man go. I've got to talk to him."

I sprinted past her and I was going full-tilt when I realized the finish line was not as close as I thought it was. And I was sprinting. I was going full-out. I was losing steam. But the finish line still wasn't any closer. But I had to keep going, didn't I?

The girl was behind me, she was seeing everything that was going on, so I kept pushing and kept pushing and kept pushing until finally I was through the finish line!

There I was, hunched over; gasping for breath when here comes... my breakfast. Not a pretty sight, I have to tell you.

As I'm there, trying to catch my breath, trying not to choke on my vomit, the girl jogs by me. And one of the race officials comes up and goes "Excuse me, sir. The finish line is over there."

Needless to say, I did <u>not</u> talk to that girl.

Before we continue on with the last step in the G.A.M.E. plan...you guessed it...some quotes on Motivation!

People often say that motivation doesn't last. Well, neither does bathing - that's why we recommend it daily. -Zig Ziglar

Motivation is the art of getting people to do what you want them to do because they want to do it.
                                              -Dwight D. Eisenhower

If people take anything from my music, it should be motivation to know that anything is possible as long as you keep working at it and don't back down.   -Eminem

Wanting something is not enough. You must hunger for it. Your motivation must be absolutely compelling in order to overcome the obstacles that will invariably come your way.
                                              -Les Brown

People need motivation to do anything. I don't think human beings learn anything without desperation.   -Jim Carrey

A champion needs a motivation above and beyond winning.   -Pat Riley

Figure Out Some Motivation

1. Find some Motivation
       Determine what works for you best, audio, visual or a combination of both.

2. Tell a good friend
       Find a goal partner and hold each other accountable

3. Surround yourself with quotes
       Find some quotes that speak to you and print them out to display at your office or home.

Chapter 4
The 1 Thing That Can Mean the Difference Between Success & Failure

Evaluation. This is the last step in our G.A.M.E. plan. You've got your goal clearly defined with a deadline. You know what action steps you're going to be taking, you have a list of them. You know what motivation you're going to be using to get this goal of yours done.

The last step, evaluation, is probably one of the most important steps. It's the one step most people don't do when it comes to goal getting and goal setting. They don't evaluate everything that they're doing to see if it's working or not.

If the actions you're taking aren't working, why are you doing them? You need to change them. If the motivation you're using is being counterproductive and it's de-motivating you, you need to change it.

What about your goal? Maybe your goal is not a realistic goal. If you don't evaluate it you'll never know that, will you?

What do you evaluate? You evaluate everything. The first step is to evaluate the goal. Take a look at this goal that you have. Is it a realistic goal? In other words, the deadline that you've set, is it obtainable? Is it a deadline that you can get?

If you set the deadline of "next week I want to lose 50 pounds," you're probably not going to get it. And you're just setting yourself up for failure. You don't want to do that, do you?

Look at your goal and your deadline and see if it's realistic or not. If it's not a realistic goal, if it's not a realistic deadline, then perhaps you need to adjust the deadline.

Look at it in a realistic manner. An easy way to do this is just do the math. If you have a certain amount of time you want to get this goal done, and a certain amount of weight, or a certain amount of money, or a certain amount of pages written in your novel, then do the math.

Divide that number of things you want by the number of weeks you have in your deadline. Then you can see what it would take each week for you to be successful, then you can see if it's realistic or not.

True Story

Several years ago I was in Japan, doing a gig, for a month. I had a lot of free time while I was there and wanted to put it to good use.

One of my goals was to transcribe a notebook of ideas onto my computer. These were ideas I'd come up with over the years and put down into a journal. The papers were getting old, some of it had gotten wet and I didn't want to risk losing it.

My deadline was to have this completed before I returned to the U.S. I had exactly 28 days to accomplish this.

I knew there were 115 pages of notes, so that worked out to about 4 pages a day to transcribe. By breaking it down, into smaller more manageable bites, then it would be easy.

I now knew that my deadline was reasonable, I could type up those 4 pages a day easily.

Again, don't set yourself up for failure. Don't give yourself that excuse of, "Well, I tried, but it just didn't work, so now I don't ever have to try again, do I?" No. That's not you. You wouldn't be reading this book otherwise.

How about the goal itself? Why not evaluate the goal? See if it's realistic. See if it's obtainable. Now, I'm all for shooting for the stars, don't get me wrong. But if your goal is to become Brad Pitt by next week, it's not very realistic.

As a matter of fact, you may want to seek psychological help. That's all I'm saying. I'm not judging. I'm just saying.

Look at your goal. See if it's realistic. A great way to do that is to see if anyone else has done this. Has anyone else done what you want to do? Now has anyone else done that in the time frame that you want to do.

Look at your abilities. If your goal is to be Brad Pitt, and you're a 95-year-old woman then that's probably not going to happen. Again, why would somebody do something like this? It's to justify to themselves, "I tried, but it didn't work. Wah wah! Boo hoo! Give me sympathy now."

The Actions

After evaluating your goal, evaluate the action steps that you're taking. See if they're working, or see if they're not working. And this is a great way to gauge everything that you're doing.

After working on your goal for a week or two, evaluate everything in the plan. Evaluate to see what's working and to see what's not working. And then, ideally what you want to do is do more of what's working and cut out what's not working. Brilliant idea, huh?

A magic formula for success: do more of what works; do less of what doesn't work. Hey, I'm not a genius. It's just common sense, right? But sometimes we don't think like that, do we? We miss the whole concept of that, because nobody every told us to evaluate what we're doing, did they? No. So evaluate everything! See if it's working or not.

It's been said that the clinical definition of insanity is to do something the exact same way over and over again, but expect a different result. That truly is insane, if you ask me. Why would you expect a different result if you haven't changed anything?

Salespeople do this all the time. When they send out a sales letter or sales email, they do a split test. They change one thing in that letter, and they send one letter out to a hundred people, the other letter out to another hundred people, and they see which one gets the better results.

But they only change one thing, because if they change more than one thing, they don't know what made the difference. They don't know what it was that made more people buy this letter than that letter.

When you're evaluating everything, make sure that you just change the things that aren't working. Maybe you need to tweak those things. Maybe it's just a little adjustment. You don't have to completely eliminate those things, but you need to adjust them. If they're working, but not as well as they should be, then adjust them. Change what you're doing. If it's not working, change it.

Your action steps: look at the steps that you're taking. Are they working? Are they not? Again, if they're not working, change them. If they are working, try to replicate them.

The Motivation

The next thing to evaluate is the motivation that you're using. Is it working or is it not? Is it motivating you or is just irritating you? Are you ignoring this motivation?

Have you put this goal of yours up in your bathroom mirror, and yet you never really even look at it? You never acknowledge it. You don't even see it. Well, then it's not working for you, is it?

Maybe you need to hear your goal every day. Record it. Play it in your car when you drive to work or when you're just driving around town. Maybe you need to have some sort of physical manifestation of this goal that you have.

Maybe your goal is to get a new car. Well, buy a model of the car that you want and have it sitting on your desk. Have it on your nightstand, so it's the first thing you see in the morning and the last thing you see before you go to bed at night. Just have it there as a constant reminder. Use it as a motivator.

See if the motivation is being counterproductive. Is it de-motivating you? Are you getting frustrated, because you see

this goal every day and go, "Okay. Yeah. Yeah.
I know. I haven't gotten around to it. I feel
horrible. Oh, my gosh. I just can't do this.
I'm a terrible person. Forget it! I just quit!"
Well, if that's the case, then adjust what
you've put there.

Change what your motivation is. Maybe
it's not the goal statement. Maybe it's some
positive quote that you can put up there.
Maybe it's something that you can look at daily
to encourage yourself to go after your goals,
and then later on you can look at this goal that
you've written down, and go after it with full
gusto as it were.

When To Evaluate

I would recommend that you evaluate
your goal, your action, and the motivation that
you're using as much as you can.

If you set yourself a one week goal then
after two days look at your progress. See if
you're getting any headway on this goal or not.

If you've fallen behind, then you know
you have to increase the action steps; you
have to do more to get this goal done within a
week. If it's a one month goal, maybe once a

week you evaluate what you're doing and if it's working or not.

You don't want to over-evaluate. I used to do this all the time. Whenever I had a weight-loss goal, I would start my diet and start my exercising, and then every day, I'd step on the scale in the morning and look. "Did I lose any weight since yesterday?" Well, yeah, maybe I did lose a little bit, but it's not real motivating, is it?

You're not seeing that big progress. So I would wait. I would wait at least a week before stepping on that scale. Matter of fact, I still do that today.

Currently, I actually have a weight-loss goal in mind, and so I'm tracking my progress. I'm seeing the results. I can look back over the last few weeks and see how much I've lost or how much I've gained back or how much I've just maintained.

But I'm evaluating my goal. I'm keeping track, and I'm keeping track of the progress in a very timely manner, not every single day. Because if I do that, it's going to de-motivate me. It's going to depress me. "I'm not losing any weight. Oh, my gosh. I'll just quit. Where's those cookies?" No. So when you're evaluating, make sure that it's a proper time frame.

When You're Done

Once you've completed your goal, evaluate everything again. "What do you mean? My goal's already done. Why would I want to evaluate?"

Look at all the steps that you've taken, all the motivation that you've used throughout this goal of yours. You've got your goal, you've achieved it. Here's a blueprint for doing exactly this goal.

Look at the steps that were most effective.
Look at the steps that were the least effective. Now, if you ever have a goal like this again or maybe this same exact goal...

But now, if you have this blueprint, you've already done it in the past, whenever you have this goal again, you can just take a look at it and follow this blueprint for success.

Maybe you can share this blueprint with a friend; somebody that has a similar goal, somebody who maybe years from now comes up to you and goes, "How did you do it? You are doing exactly what I want to do. How did you do it all those years ago?"

Rather than just sitting there and thinking back, trying to remember, you can pull out this blueprint that you have for success and share it with them.

Share it with them, and they will love you for it, because you've just taken the learning curve off of what they want to do. You've saved them countless hours and days and weeks and months, maybe even years of trying and failing as it were.

And then, if you have a goal that is similar to this goal, maybe it's a business-type goal, it's a physical fitness goal, you're goal was to run a marathon. Now you want to compete in a triathlon. You can use the same blueprint again and help you get this goal as well.

Evaluate everything that you're doing and see if it's working. If it's not, change it. If it is, do more of it.

True genius resides in the capacity for evaluation of uncertain, hazardous, and conflicting information.
                    -Winston Churchill

Fear cannot be banished, but it can be calm and without panic; it can be mitigated by reason and evaluation.
                    -Vannevar Bush

A Truthful Evaluation Of Yourself Gives Feedback For Growth and Success
                    -Brenda Johnson Padgitt

Thoughts, quotes, and philosophies— good or bad—cause us to evaluate ourselves. And that is good.
                    -Richelle E. Goodrich

Evaluation Time

1. Evaluate your goal
   Determine if it's realistic and if the deadline is reasonable or not.

2. Evaluate the actions
   See if the actions you're taking are working or not. If they're not change them! If they are working; do more of them!
3. Evaluate the Motivators
   Are you being motivated by what you're using? Is it irritating you? Do you hardly notice it? Then try something different!

Chapter 5
Purpose, Passion, Practice & Planning

The four P's to going beyond good enough. The four P's stand for purpose, passion, plan and practice. Let's start with the first one.

Your Purpose

When you set a goal, you need to discover what the purpose of this goal is, what is the reason why you are going after this goal?

It sounds kind of simplistic, but it's not because it's usually not the first reason that comes up.

If your goal is to lose weight, you want to look better, that's your goal, that's the purpose behind it. You want to make more money, that's the purpose behind this goal of starting your own business, or creating a new product or writing a book.

But when it comes down to it, is that really the purpose behind it? I don't think so. That is the result of the goal. The goal is, you want to make more money, you want to have more money, that's the purpose right? You want to be rich. No, you don't want more money,

What? That's crazy talk Fred. No, you don't want more money. You want the feelings associated with having more money. If you have more money than you feel more secure, you feel confident because you can provide for your family.

You feel generous because you have enough money to give to charity. You have security. The feeling that you get when you have more money is the purpose behind that money goal of yours. The purpose isn't to get rich, the purpose is to get those feelings associated with being rich.

The same thing can be said of the weight loss goal. You want to become healthier. Well, that is a great purpose to have behind this goal. You want to be healthier, you want to live longer.

But what is the true purpose? Are you alone and you're thinking that maybe if you lose weight, you'll be more attractive to somebody else and you'll be able to get somebody in your life? That's the purpose behind that goal.

Again, it's the emotion, the feeling behind the goal that you have. That is the true purpose of the goal. Maybe your weight loss goal is you do want to be healthier because you want to live longer.

I know in my case, I just started a goal of mine; I cut out sugar and I cut out gluten from my diet. Now at the time in this writing I'm 48 years old and I have a 16 month old daughter. The purpose of my goal is not to get healthier. That's a byproduct, that's a result. The whole purpose behind it in my mind is I want to dance at my daughter's wedding someday.

At the rate I'm going, being 48 years old and she's just over a year old now, it's going to be, I hope at least 20 years before she gets married, probably more than that. So I'll be in my 70's by the time she does decide to get married.

So, am I going to be in the best health? Not if I keep on with the sugar and the gluten. So my purpose behind the weight loss goal is exactly that. I want to dance at my daughter's wedding someday.

If you discover the true purpose behind your goal, that will help you as a motivator. It will keep you going forward with this goal of yours. Now if the goal of yours is not your goal, if this was a goal that was given to you by your boss or significant other, something along those lines, then discovering the purpose behind this is probably even more important, than if it's your goal because if it's your goal, then it's personal, it is something that you want.

But if this deadline was set to you by your boss, "Look by the end of the month, you need to have your sales numbers are up by 20%." Well what's the purpose behind this? You are going to get fired. That's a result of you not getting this goal; that's not the purpose behind it.

The purpose behind this goal is for you to become a better salesperson. For you to work harder, to find more prospects, to figure out exactly what it is that you are doing right and do more of it. Figure out what is wasting your time when it comes to your job and eliminating that.

That's the purpose of that goal, now that goal is more personal to you, it's more concrete, because it has an outcome other than, "I'm not going to get fired." If you're constantly living in fear of losing your job, you're probably not going to be that happy are you?

So any goal that you are given, you can discover for yourself a purpose behind it that has meaning to you.

Passion

When you discover the purpose behind your goal, then you can make it your passion. Because like I said, maybe this goal is not your passion. Maybe this goal is not something you really want to do but you have to do it. Maybe you have to do it for health reasons; maybe you have to do it for work reasons.

Maybe you have to do it because you know if you don't do it, you're going to die. I hope that's not a work-related goal because then it sounds like you work for the mob.

Once you've made this goal personal and your goal, you can discover the passion of this goal. You can discover what it's going to take for you to love this goal, to really want to make this goal happen.

This is so important when it's not your goal because you don't have a whole lot of motivation to make it happen, other than what I mentioned before, getting fired, being nagged by your significant other, things like that.

Make this goal your passion. If nothing else, the passion behind your goal could be just to get it done, to have set a goal and have made it happen. To have achieved something in your life, something that you didn't think you could do.

Something that perhaps other people didn't think you were going to be able to do.

That's why they gave you this goal. They didn't want to challenge you, they wanted to see you fail. Now your passion can be to prove them wrong. To hold up this goal achieved in their face and just defiantly laugh at them. "You didn't think I could do it. Did you? Look, I did it." Discover your passion.

Maybe this goal you have is your passion and that's great because now you have even that much more going on for you. It's your goal, it's personal, it's a passion you have, and it's something that you have always wanted to do.

But is passion alone going to get you there? No, but it will help you to keep on track;

it will help to motivate you. Because this is something that you want to do, something you want to have otherwise you wouldn't have set this goal. Now if it's a passion of yours, and you haven't already done it, then maybe you are not as passionate about it as you thought you were.

Maybe you need to discover why you are passionate about this goal. Again, we go back to the purpose. Why are you so fired up about this goal? Why are you passionate about it? Is it the goal itself specifically or is it the purpose, the by-product of it?

Once you start this company of yours, you are going to be able to make three quarters of $1 million a year and donate two thirds of that to charity. So now you've discovered that the passion is donating, is being charitable, that's the passion behind this. Once you have the purpose and you have the passion, you are leaps and bounds ahead of everyone else trying to get their goals are achieved.

Planning

You have got a G.A.M.E. plan, don't you? I hope you read the other part of this book, about the G.A.M.E. plan, haven't you? You have a goal, you are taking action, you are motivating yourself and you are evaluating to see if it's working on not.

You have a plan in place and you are doing what 98% of the people in the world don't do when it comes to their goals, you are doing something about it, you're taking some action aren't you?

You are, aren't you? You should be, I know you want to get through this book but trust me; you can take action once you take a break from this chapter.

Success doesn't happen by accident. Plan on success, plan out what exactly is that you're going to do, make a plan and write it down. I'm really big on writing things down, I mean, pen and paper. Pencil and paper, crayons, whatever you have, write it down.

Instead of typing it on your computer or your mobile device or whatever, write it down because when you write it triggers a part of your brain, something called the Reticular Activating System.

That's a big fancy word for, the part of your brain that makes something real. When you write down your plan, when you write down your goals, it locks it into your brain; it makes it real to you.

Have you ever written something down so you don't forget it? 90% of the time, you don't have to look at what you've written to remember it. It's locked in your brain because you wrote it down.

When you make a plan, write it down. Sketch out a plan, doesn't have to be perfect the first time.

Just brainstorm, right down a plan, start writing down ideas, action steps that you are going to take, people you are going to contact, groups you're going to join, motivations that you are going to be using. Get specific with this goal of yours, set deadlines and write it all down.

Once you've got it written down, then you can go through it, you can edit it, you can figure out what steps need to be taken first, what steps need to be taken last, what steps don't need to be taken at all.

Some of these ideas might not work at all, but plan on it, make a plan and then put it into place. Take some action, schedule your time.

Again, don't leave success to chance, it's not going to just fall in your lap, you have to be prepared for it, you have to plan on it.

Most people that are "overnight successes" spent at least 20 years getting ready to become overnight successes. It's not that they were just suddenly thrust upon the world and were successful.

No, they've been preparing, they have been working on their craft, they've been studying, they've been writing, they've been doing whatever it is that they do to get ready, to make their debut in the world.

Plan out your week, plan out your months and plan out your year.

Take some time at the beginning of every week and plan what it is that you are going to do that week to make your goals happen. Start with the week and look at the things you have to do, the "must dos" for that week.

You have to go to work, you have to pick the kids up from school, you have to run errands, you have doctor's appointments. Schedule all that first and see where it is that you can fit in some of these action steps for your goals.

If you have a lot of goals, you may have to push some of them together. You may have to make better use of your time, manage your time better as it were.

But just plan out your week, figure out where it is and what it is you are going to be doing on each specific day. If you can plan it down to the hour, that's great.

If you are the type of person that needs to plan every single moment, go ahead and do that. But don't spend too much time doing it because then all you'll be doing is planning on success and you won't be doing anything about this success. Plan on it and then take some action.

Which leads us to the final P. No, that's not a bathroom break. I'm talking about;

Practice

My background is in entertainment, so I know the importance of practice. If you play a musical instrument, if you play any sort of sports, you know how important practice is, don't you?

You were not just born good at something. Maybe you had an aptitude for it, but you did have to practice in order to get better at it.

It works the same way with goals and goal setting, think about it. If you set a goal and you try to do something and it doesn't work, you may quit, you may forget about it, "It just doesn't work for me, I tried and it's not going to work."

It's an old tune sung by so many people around the world. "I tried to do something and it didn't work, so I quit." You know the old expression right, "If at first you don't succeed... quit." That's not how it used to go but, that's how most people think nowadays.

But the first time you try to walk when you were a little baby, it probably didn't work. It took a little practice. First time you tried to ride a bike or swim, probably didn't work and you did practice at it. Why should getting your goals be any different than that?

If you go about your goal and you get it the first try, well first of all, good for you. But second of all, maybe that wasn't a big goal, maybe that wasn't a huge goal. You got it so easily; maybe it wasn't enough of a challenge for you.

Maybe your goal was, "I'm going to get out of bed today." And it's a great goal, especially if you are depressed. But maybe that's not enough for you.

Maybe you are afraid that you are going to have to practice this goal of yours, before you get it right. You are going to have to "fail" over and over again before you achieve success. Maybe you are afraid that other people are going to see you fail at this goal of yours.

Well too bad, because it's going to happen either way. Either they're going to see you fail at trying to do something, or they're going to see you <u>as</u> a failure for not trying anything.

Personally, I would rather try and fail and try and fail and keep on trying, than to not try anything at all.

In most cases, the person that stands there and laughs at you because you failed usually is not doing anything with their life. Okay, they're doing one thing; they're motivating you to make this goal of yours happen so that you can stick it in their face.

I had a great experience with practice. Again, my background is in entertainment.

True Story

As a kid, I had gone to this theme park and I had seen magicians perform there. I always used to think to myself, "Someday, that's going to be me."

Well three years after I saw my first magician at the park, I got hired as the magician there. I got hired and I was up there on stage doing my thing. Now the interesting thing is, I was doing a lot of shows over the summer. It was a four-month period and I was doing pretty much six shows a day, six days a week for four months. Six times six is 36. Four months, that's about 16 weeks. That is 576 shows in four months.

Now this is back in the late '80s. Yes, I'm old and I've videotaped my show. It was beta actually. I've videotaped my show at the beginning of the summer when I first started the job and then I've videotaped the end of the summer and I watched them back-to-back.

I compared what my show was like at the beginning of the summer and what it was like at the end. I have to tell you, it was like night and day. I was basically doing the same tricks, the same effects, but the way I did them was so vastly different. I had polished the routines to a shine because I had done them over and over again.

I had done 576 shows in four months. That's more shows than most of the people I knew at the time, magicians did in five years, let alone four months. And during those four months, I had learned a lot.

Anything and everything that could go wrong in the show did at one time or another. And I learned how to either fix that problem so it would never happen again, or I learned how to deal with that problem and move on with the show. How to solve the problem during the show, how to make fun of it or how to ignore it. I learned a lot because I got a lot of practice that summer.

Whatever skill set that you need to make this goal of yours happen, practice it, practice it and refine it, evaluate the practice that you're doing and see if you're making progress, see if you're getting better or not. Set yourself benchmarks as it were and make sure that you are improving on what you're doing.

If you're not improving, evaluate, see if you can change what it is that you are doing to get some improvement on this. Use the four P's when it comes to goal setting and goal getting. Discover the purpose, let that purpose strive your passion. Plan exactly what it is that you are going to do and then practice the skills that you need, to make this goal of yours happen.

Productivity is never an accident. It is always the result of a commitment to excellence, intelligent planning, and focused effort.
-Paul J. Meyer

Without leaps of imagination, or dreaming, we lose the excitement of possibilities. Dreaming, after all, is a form of planning.
-Gloria Steinem

Every great dream begins with a dreamer. Always remember, you have within you the strength, the patience, and the passion to reach for the stars to change the world.
-Harriet Tubman

There is no passion to be found playing small - in settling for a life that is less than the one you are capable of living.
                    -Nelson Mandela

The purpose of education is to replace an empty mind with an open one.
                    -Malcolm Forbes

Develop a passion for learning. If you do, you will never cease to grow.
                    -Anthony J. D'Angelo

Efforts and courage are not enough without purpose and direction.
                    -John F. Kennedy

I've always considered myself to be just average talent and what I have is a ridiculous insane obsession for practice and preparation.   -Will Smith

Work the Four P's

1. Find your Purpose
   Discover the true purpose of your goals, what's behind them

2. Find your Passion
   What can you do to really "own" this goal, to make it a driving force in your life?

3. Make a plan
   Don't leave your success to chance, plan exactly what you'll be doing

4. Practice your skills
   Whatever skills you need to complete your goals practice at them so they become second nature.

Chapter 6
Changing Your Mindset

When it comes to setting goals and getting goals, your mindset is very, very, important. Henry Ford is famous for saying,

"Whether you think you can do something or whether you think you can't do something, you are right."

I'm not talking about positive thinking and thinking only good thoughts and sending out those vibes in the world where if I just think good things and think about all the good things I want to have happen they are going to automatically happen to me.

I'm talking about your mindset. How you go into setting goals. How you think about things. About the people that you interact with, the input that they have in your brains every day and the effect on your mindset.

Never Fail Again

The first thing I want to talk about is failure. That is a huge obstacle when it comes to getting your goals. People are afraid of failing. And why is that? Well typically, when you fail, and it's in a public arena you are ridiculed for it.

Think about it. You are out there trying to skate, you fall down and your friends laugh at you. You try to be good at sports, play a little baseball, you don't catch the ball, people ridicule you, because you failed.

We are almost programmed as a society to denounce failure, to look at failure as a bad thing. You've tried it and you failed. I failed at my marriage. I failed to do a good job and I got fired. Well, there is another way to look at failure.

Whenever you try and do something, one of two things is going to happen. It's going to work, or is not going to work. That's pretty much it. It's either going to work, or is not going to work.

Either you going to succeed or you are going to fail. It's black and white. Now I know there are some grey areas, where it might kind of work, might kind of not work. But stick with me here.

If you change your mindset about failure, then it won't affect you in a negative way. I'm going to tell you about a very important day in my life. It was August 24th 1994. That was the last day I ever failed. The last day I ever failed at anything.

Does that mean I've succeeded at everything I've done? No. But that was the day I discovered as long as I got a result, I didn't fail. As long as some outcome came out of this, I didn't fail. I got a result.

It may have not been the result that I wanted but I got a result. Something happened. Now I've learned. I've learned how not to do this.

There is an old story about Thomas Edison. He was trying to create a new type of a battery and he was being interviewed by a reporter. The reporter knew that he had failed over 10,000 times trying to perfect this battery.

When asked how does it feel to fail so many times? He said, "I haven't failed. I just discovered 10,000 ways that don't work."

True Story

One July I was trying to create some wooden gears. I was creating an illusion that needed a series of gears. I didn't know where to get gears so I decided I'm going to make some.

I don't know if you know anything about gears. But they need to mesh precisely in order for them to work properly.

So I experimented. I spent the day failing. That's how some people will look at it. I spent the day failing. All day long I made some gears; they didn't work. I made some more gears; those didn't work. I made two more, those didn't work. I kept changing things, changing things.

People look at that and think I spent the day failing. No, I spent about 12 hours that day learning how not to make a wooden gear.

But something magically happened. At the end of that day, I found out how to make a wooden gear. How did I do that? By failing all day long I was discovering ways that didn't work.

Did you know that scientists love failure? They embrace failure. You talk to anybody that works in research and development and failure is a big important part of the process. Because if you are not failing a bunch of times then that means you are not trying.

The whole key to overcoming a failure is to keep on trying. We've all heard the phrase. If at first you don't succeed try, try, again.

If you keep on trying something the same way over and over again and don't change what you are doing, then you are not going to get a different result, you are going to get the same result.

It's been said that the clinical definition of insanity is to try something again and again the exact same way but expect a different result. That's crazy talk, literally crazy talk.

If you are trying something and it doesn't work, change it. If that's not working, change it again. Keep on trying. Keep on quote "failing" until you get the result that you want.

See this is where the motivation aspect of the G.A.M.E. plan comes into to play. Because if you are trying something and you are not getting the result that you want, how many times are you going to keep on trying?

Until you get the result? Well, if you don't have some form of motivator behind you, you are probably going to quit early on.

But since you do have some motivation, you have a prize at the end of the goal. Then you are going to keep on going until you get the result that you want.

So many people quit. They stop just shy of success because they don't know how close they are to getting what they want. They are just looking at all the failures. They are not looking at the process. You are learning. You are improving. You are trying different things. Until you get the result that you want.

This is why the evaluation portion of the game plan is so important. When you are evaluating what you are doing you are seeing if it's working or not.

If you're keeping track of it, when you get the result that you want, and later on you want to do this again, you've got a plan.

You can call it your master plan. Here is everything you tried that didn't work and here is the stuff that did work. You have a plan for success!

To quote the great movie Apollo thirteen, failure is not an option. Don't look at the failure. Look at the results that you get.

Resistance

Resistance can be a good thing. When you are weight training, there is resistance training. You are putting stress on your muscles. There is some resistance there and you are building that muscle up to make it stronger.

Resistance fighters in history are known as the underdogs and the heroes of the revolution. The people that made it happen. They're resistance fighters because they are resisting the status quo. They are heroes.

But there is another form of resistance. Resistance in the form of self doubt, Resistance in the form of that little voice in your head that tells you, you are not good enough.

There is a great book called the War of Art by Steven Pressfield (not the Art of War by Sun Tzu). I recommend you pick up this book. It's a quick easy read, but it is a great read.

In it he talks about the artist and what keeps them from producing the work that is inside them.

Now this all does apply to you regular folk out there too. But he is talking mainly about the artist. And most artists come upon Resistance. We doubt ourselves. We don't think we are good enough most of the time. Our work is not the best it can be, so we don't want to show it to anyone. This is Resistance. It's not just for the artists out there. It's for everybody.

When you are trying to do something you haven't done before, there is a part of your brain that wants to protect you. That subconscious part of your brain that says if you do this, you might fail.

You might be embarrassed because you're spending all this money and you are going to lose your house or you are trying something that no one has ever done before. You are trying something that you've never done before and you may not be successful.

So that Resistance pops up. And it tells you, "Are you sure you want to do this? You might get hurt. You know you are probably not smart enough to make this happen. "

"You know, other people have tried this and they failed and they were smarter than you."

You are not good enough. You are not smart enough. And doggone it, people don't like you. (Thank you Stuart Smalley)

Resistance pops up in many different forms. Is not just the little voice in your head that tells you you're not good enough, it's also;

Procrastination

I'll do that later. I don't need to do that right now, there's more important things that I have to do than starting my own business. I have to go make sure that all the shampoos in my bathroom are lined up in alphabetical order.

That's more important than starting my own business, isn't it? I have to go clean my own toilet instead of answering all those emails.

Instead of making those sales calls, I know I'm going to straighten up my desk. Procrastination is another form of Resistance.

When you're constantly coming up with "other" things to do beside tackle this goal of yours that's procrastination and Resistance.

True Story

Somebody once loaned me a book on how to stop procrastinating and I never got around to reading it. Seriously.

Another form of resistance is perfection, waiting for everything to be just right before you start the process, before you launch your business, before you submit you book to be published.

Everything has to be perfect; I have to have the right tools. It has to look right. Everything has to be perfect.

It's been said that a product that is 80% completed and released will do so much better than a product that is 99% done but never released.

Well, duh, think about that. A product that is 1% complete is going to do better if it's been released than a product that is a hundred percent done but never released.

Do you know how many novels are sitting in people's laptops, their hard drives, their desk drawers because it's not perfect yet?

I don't want to release it is not perfect. I don't want to start this business because the business climate is not right. The economy has to bounce back before I start this business.

Everything has to be perfect before you want to go for this goal of yours. Well guess what? That's never going to happen.

Everything is never going to be perfect. There is no perfection. There is only right now. When is the perfect time to do whatever it is that you wanted to do? Five minutes ago.

No, that's not an excuse. Well the time is already up, so I guess I better not do it. No, that means do it now. Don't procrastinate. Don't wait for perfection. And fight the resistance.

The Influencers

Another factor in your mind-set has to do with people in your life, the people that influence you day in and day out.

Are they positive minded people? Are they negative minded people? Are they the kind of people that will sit there and look at you when you tell them that big goal of yours they go, "Dude you can't do that. What are you serious? What are you nuts? You are just going to waste your time. That's all you're going to do. You are wasting your time and you'll never be able to do that."

Why do these people do this? They are your friends right? They are your co-workers maybe. Maybe even your family.

I think, consciously, they are not doing that to try to keep you down, to try to harm you. They are trying to keep you <u>from</u> harm. They don't want to see you go out there and fail and be ridiculed.

But subconsciously I think, maybe they are thinking to themselves, "Okay if you go out and try this and succeed, that means it can be done, and I have no excuse for the way my life is, because you are getting what you want and I'm not. So I can't let you do that and be successful because then I'm going to feel bad about myself."

I've no data to back that up. I just learned that from experience. I know that there are people out there that don't want to see me succeed. Because it means that they haven't been successful. And if I can do it, well, they should be able to do it too.

It's been said that you are influenced by the top five people around you. If you surround yourself with people that are constantly telling you can't do it, you can't do it.

Well guess what, you need to get away from these people. Get away from these people and make new friends. Make new friends or just take what they are saying with a grain of salt.

Take it as a challenge. Oh yes, you don't think I can do this? Oh watch me. If you do that, more than likely, something is going to happen. You are going to lose that friend because they don't want to see you successful.

But guess what, you are going to make new friends. You are going to find like-minded people, people that are positive minded like you. People that are "go getter's", that know how to set goals and get their goals. So surround yourself with positive minded people.

Your vocabulary

How you talk about things is very, very, important, in the whole going beyond good enough process. Saying that you wish you had something, or you want something is not going to make it happen. Remember my grandma used to say "Wish in one hand and spit in the other and see which one fills up first."

So, instead of saying I want something, or I wish I had something, change it. Change it to I will have this. This *will* happen. I <u>will</u> make this happen.

Change the way that you speak and the way you talk about your goals. Don't think to yourself, "I don't think I can do this." Think to yourself, "I <u>know</u> I can do this." It sounds simplistic.

It can be very difficult at times because you are thinking, "really seriously I don't think I can do this." If you have it set in your brain, I don't think I can do this, well then change it up.

Just think to yourself, well if I did know what to do, what would I do? All right, I can't do it, that's fine. But if I did know what to do, what would I do? I learned that from Tony Robbins.

By the way, if you haven't read any of Tony Robbins stuff, or listened to any of it, I urge you to go do that. Not right now, finish reading this book and later on, go find Tony Robbins.

Ask the right questions, not why I can't;
but instead why I <u>will</u> get this goal of mine.

True Story

Back when I was single I'd go out to night clubs to meet women. It usually didn't work out for me.

My usual attitude wasn't one of confidence, my opening line was: "you don't want to dance with me do you?"

Ok not really, but that was the mindset I had, no confidence at all.

One night I decided to change that. I came up with a line that was full of confidence and bravado.

I went up to a girl and said "Don't just stand there, dance with me!"

She looked me up and down and said "No!" Really pushing my self confidence I replied "oh come on...dance with me".

To which I got "Nooooooo, go away!"

It's a wonder I ever got married!

You need to overcome the tug of people against you as you reach for high goals.
-George S. Patton

Ability is what you're capable of doing. Motivation determines what you do. Attitude determines how well you do it.
-Raymond Chandler

Choosing to be positive and having a grateful attitude is going to determine how you're going to live your life.
-Joel Osteen

Nothing can stop the man with the right mental attitude from achieving his goal; nothing on earth can help the man with the wrong mental attitude.
-Thomas Jefferson

Your attitude, not your aptitude, will determine your altitude.
-Zig Ziglar

A positive attitude causes a chain reaction of positive thoughts, events and outcomes. It is a catalyst and it sparks extraordinary results.
-Wade Boggs

The greatest day in your life and mine is when we take total responsibility for our attitudes. That's the day we truly grow up.
-John C. Maxwell

Ways to Change Your Mindset

1. Never fail again
   Change the way you perceive "failure" and look at the results you get instead

2. Fight the Resistance
   Recognize the different forms of Resistance in your life and negate it

3. Procrastinate Later
   Tackle those tasks right now that you've been putting off

4. Who's Influencing You?
   Take a look at the people in your life to see what kind of impact they're having on you (good or bad)

5. Change Your Vocabulary
   Stop thinking about how you "can't" and begin thinking about how you "can" and "will" complete your goals

Chapter 7
How To Make It All Work

Business applications

How can you make all of these tools work for your business? It doesn't take much of stretch to figure that out, does it? Use the G.A.M.E. plan when it comes to your sales goals, when it comes to your business goals.

You want to start a business, clearly define this goal of yours. What is the business going to be all about? Where is it going to be located? What exactly is it that you're going to be doing? Clearly define your goal.

I want to start a new business. Great, when are you going to do it? Set a deadline. Clearly define it, state it in the past tense. As of this date, I have started this new business and I am on my way to being successful.

Then take some action. Find out what is it you need to do to start this new business. Do you need to incorporate? Do you need to get an LLC? Do you need a business license? What steps do you need to take to launch this business of yours?

What are you going to use to motivate yourself to continue on with this business? It's said that most businesses fold within the first year. What are you going to do to make sure that won't happen to you? How are you going to keep yourself motivated?

Set a time when you're going to evaluate the steps that you're taking; the goal itself. When are you going to evaluate to see whether it's working or not?

If your goal is a sales goal, use the same formula. Set the goal. Get more sales. That's not a clearly defined specific goal, is it?

No. Make it a clear goal. We're going to increase sales by 20%. That's pretty clear but it's not specific enough. How many more sales are you going to make in your timeframe?

Is it a week goal? Perhaps you need to make 2 more sales this week. If you're selling cars, that's a great goal. If you're selling washers, maybe that's not a great goal, unless you're selling a whole bunch of washers.

Make your sales goal a specific goal. We are going to do this much more in sales. We are going to have X-amount of sales by this time.

Make sure it's a realistic goal. Don't set your goal as, 'We're going to sell 50 more cars today.' Could that happen? Sure. Is it realistic? Probably not, not unless you're selling cars by the shipload.

Make sure your goal is realistic. Make sure the deadline is a realistic deadline. You want to motivate your sales staff but you don't want to depress your sales staff. You don't want to have all that pressure hanging over them.

Keep yourself motivated. Keep your sales staff motivated by clearly defining the actions that you're going to be taking. Get together with your sales staff and brainstorm action steps to increase your sales.

If you just tell your salespeople, "Here is our goal for this month. Each of you are going to bring in 5 more customers. You're going to sell 5 more cars by the end of the month."

Brainstorm. Bring all the salespeople and say, "Here's our goal: I want each of you to bring in 5 more sales by the end of the month. How do you think we can do this?"

Again, don't use the motivation as, 'If you don't, you're going to be fired.' That may work in some instances but it's probably not going to be a very good healthy work environment. Instead brainstorm.

Make a list: 50 ways to increase sales this month. Have everyone come up make their own list. Don't do it all together at once. Everyone sit down and make a list of 50 ways. They may not be able to come up with 50 ways, but they can come up with 20 or 30 ways, hopefully. If you have 4, 5, 10 sales staff, then you've just come up with more than 50 ways on how to increase the sales.

Make sure that they're not stuck in the same old mindset of 'This is the way you make a sale. This is how you do it.' No. Brainstorm. Think of crazy ideas. How can you bring more customers in?

Don't do the standard 'We'll dress up as a clown and stand by the road with a sign', because that's been done before. You can do that, sure, but come up with different ideas. You can brainstorm.

They're probably not all going to work but don't worry. Come up with some ideas. Brainstorm with your sales staff and list the action steps that you're all going to take to get this goal of yours.

Then make sure that you evaluate what's going on. Don't just look at it at the end of the month and go, "How'd you guys do? Anyone made some sales? You didn't? Great, you're all fired."

Evaluate the process as it's going on. See what's working, see what's not working, see what's bringing the customers in and see what's driving the customers away. Hopefully, they're driving in a new car. Evaluate everything that you're doing.

Don't forget the 4 P's. Discover the purpose of these sales. Why is it that they are going to get those 5 sales this month? What is it about each person that is going to drive them, make them passionate about this goal?

It's going to be different for everyone. You don't want to spend a whole lot of time on this because then no one's going to make any sales, are they? Discover what their passion is, why they want to make this goal happen and what is the plan they're going to use to get the result that they want?

What do they need to practice to make this goal happen? Is it their sales pitch? Do they need to practice that? Is it their marketing technique? Is it their response time?

Are they not getting back to the customers in the email quick enough?

Practice, plan, find the purpose, and discover their passion.

Make sure that the mindset is in the correct mode; it's a positive one. This is a goal we are going to have happen. This is a goal that we all know we can do because we have a plan. We have a list of more than 50 ways to make this happen, and our deadline is an achievable deadline. It's realistic. We can make all of this happen.

Don't forget, failure is not an option; failure is a result. The more times you fail, the closer you will be to success.

Salespeople say this all time, "Every 'no' that you get means you're one step closer to the 'yes.'" Track everything that you're doing. Look at how many 'no's' you're getting before you get that yes.

Then you can use that as guesstimate. Say that typically on average, you get 7 'no's' before you get a 'yes.' You've just gotten your fourth 'no', so statistically, you've got 3 more 'no's' before you get to a 'yes.' You're <u>that</u> close to success.

You can use everything we've talked about in this book for any business that you want. It's a universal concept that applies to all businesses:

Your G.A.M.E. plan,
Your purpose,
The passion,
The plan,
The practice,
Your mindset,
Associating with positive people.

Whatever your business is, use all of this in the book and go beyond "good enough."

Personal Application

Using all of these techniques in your personal life is simple, as well. Set your personal goals: I want to lose weight. Make them specific. Set a deadline. What action steps are you going to take to lose this weight? What is motivating you to keep on exercising and keep on dieting?

In the last few months, I decided to give up sugar and go gluten-free. I have a great reason for doing it: I've discovered the purpose of this goal of mine, the passion behind it, as it were.

I'm 48-years-old right now, and I have a 16-month-old daughter at the time of this writing. My purpose for going gluten-free and sugar-free is I want to dance at my daughter's wedding someday.

Do I know she's going to get married? No, of course not, it's just the idea that I want to be around long enough to dance at her wedding. She's not even 2-years-old at this point, if she gets married when she's 30, that means I'm going to be almost 80.

In order for me to be around that long, I need to be healthier; I need to slim down a bit, I need to drop a few pounds, I need to be in better shape. That is my purpose. That is the motivation behind the goal that I have.

That's a personal goal. It's a real goal now. There's a reason for it, I see it every day. She's my reason. Sounds cliché, but she's my reason for living. She's my reason for living better.

I want to be around when she discovers the person that she loves. I want to be there to pay for her wedding. I want to be there to look at the person she's with and judge them.

Are you any good for my daughter? I want to be around.

Discover some motivation that works for you and start using it.

Evaluate everything that you're doing. You're exercising, but you're not losing any weight. Evaluate why.

Maybe it's because after you exercise, you treat yourself to Krispy Kreme donuts.

Don't get me wrong; I love the Krispy Kreme. At least, I used to before I went sugar-and gluten-free. Please, don't mention Krispy Kreme again, you're killing me.

Maybe that's why you're not losing any weight. You're putting in the effort, but you're putting in the calories in your mouth. Evaluate everything that you're doing. Is it working? Is it not working?

You can apply this to just about anything in your personal life. You want your child to do better in school. Set yourself a goal. Use the G.A.M.E. plan.

Discover their purpose. Why do they want to do better in school? Discover what their passion is. Maybe you can tie it to their learning process. Motivate them. Use some sort of reward system.

Just make sure they're not going to resent you for not giving them that iPad because they didn't get their grades up in time.

Your relationships

Maybe you're relationship isn't where you want it to be or where it used to be. Things happen in our lives. We get married, and at first, things are hot and heavy.

Remember when you first started dating your significant other? You were really committed to this. You went out of your way to do nice things for them. You made an effort to make sure you looked good. If you've been with them for a while, maybe things have slacked off a bit.

Use your G.A.M.E. plan. Set yourself a goal: I want to look better. I want to make our relationship the way it used to be. How can I do that?

Here's my goal. I want to put the passion back into my relationship. How can we make that happen? Start making a list of action steps. Brainstorm. Do a 50-ways list: 50 ways I can improve my relationship. 50 ways I can make my significant other fall in love with me all over again.

These techniques in this book are here to help you go beyond good enough, but not just in your business, not just in the goals that you have, but in your life, as well.

You can apply this to just about anything. Use the G.A.M.E. plan. Discover the purpose. Why do you want your relationship to be like it was before? Does that mean you're going to get some more often? Maybe that is your purpose. Maybe that's your passion. See what I did there?

Practice what you need to practice. Maybe you need to practice being more attentive to your spouse. Maybe you need to practice taking time and listening to them. Maybe you need to practice helping them be who they want to be.

Make a plan, plan on improving this relationship.

My wife and I, we have a date night. Every week, we set aside, this is the time, we go out, just me and her, just the two of us and we have a nice little date. We treat ourselves to this.

I know lots of couples do this, but some have stopped doing this because life gets in the way: The kids, the job, other family members. Plan on getting this goal of yours, plan on improving your relationship.

These goals that you set, they are obviously important to you; otherwise, you wouldn't be thinking about them. They wouldn't be on your mind, would they? Use everything you've learned in the book, not just for your business, but your personal life, as well. Stop living your life just good enough, and go beyond "good enough."

Chapter 8
Exercises To Do

When it comes to getting your goals completed and getting the results that you want, sometimes you get stuck. You have your action lists, but you run out of ideas. You're sitting there and you are thinking, "What can I do to make this goal of mine happen? What can I do to turn this into a reality? What can I do to make my dreams come true? "

You're stuck and you don't know what to do. Try a little brainstorming. I like to make a list. I call it a, "50 ways list."

50 ways list

I mentioned this earlier in the book, but I know how some people like to skim over things or jump around in a book. Since this is such a useful tool I thought I'd repeat myself.

I have my goal and in this case it doesn't have to be a clearly defined specific goal but just a basic goal statement. I think to myself, "All right, what are 50 ways that I can do this?"

You make a list, 50 ways on how to do this. Fifty ways on how to make more money. Fifty ways to promote my business. Fifty ways to increase sales. Fifty ways to sell more cars.

Now why 50 ways? Well if you just set your sights at let's say 20 ways, you could probably come up with 20 ways to do just about anything. Twenty ways would be fairly simple but if you need to come up with 50 ways, 50 ways to do this task you set out then it's more of a challenge.

You're going to push yourself. You are going to start to think outside of the box. You're going to get creative with your ideas and you're going to get more specific with the ideas as well.

If your goal is to lose 20 pounds and one of the 50 ways is start exercising, now you'll get more specific. What exercises are you going to do? You're going to start jogging, you start running, you start weight training, or you're going to do a Zumba class. What exactly is it that you are going to be doing?

Here's what's going to happen. You are going to get to 30 ideas, maybe even 40 and you'll start to run out of ideas. You won't know what to do.

You'll start to come up with some crazy ideas, some silly ideas and maybe even some stupid ideas. But it's okay. Keep on writing. You want to fill that page up.

As a matter of fact don't even count them at first. Just start writing until it looks like you have around 50 because you may even come up with more than 50 ways which is great.

If you get stuck don't worry about it. If you sit there and you've got 40, you've got 30, you've got 48 and you just don't know what to do, put the list aside. Walk away from it. Go take a walk. Watch a movie. Read a book. Get your mind off of it and come back to it later. Come back with a fresh perspective.

Maybe even during this time you'll come up with some more ideas because it'll be in the back of your brain. It will be percolating back there.

For my video blog I wanted to have a blog a week so I sat down and came up with 50 blog titles, 50 subjects that I can blog on throughout the year. Now when it comes time to record those blogs I don't have to sit there and think about, "All right what am I going to talk about today?" I pull out my 50 ways list. I pick and choose.

Of course as the weeks go on I come with more ideas and I add them to the list. So now is not just a 50 ways list, it's a 60 ways list, a 70, an 80 ways list. Now I've got blog topics for many, many months in the future. I don't have to worry about it.

What about when it comes to your goals? You've got a list now –a list of 50 ways on how to do this. So go through the list. Go through the list and pick out the best ones, the ones that you think are going to get the biggest bang for your buck, the ones that are going to work immediately, the ones that are going to get the best results.

Start doing those first and get the ball rolling on this goal of yours. Implement some of those ideas immediately if you can. Then as the days go on, as the weeks go on and you're getting further and further into the goal of yours and maybe some of these things are working, some of them aren't, go back to your list. Go back to your list and try some of the other ideas.

Maybe some of the ideas are easy ideas. Maybe they are more difficult. Maybe they are outlandish ideas. But now whenever you get stuck with a goal of yours, you have this resource, you have a list of 50 ways on how to get your goal.

One hundred goals

Here's a fun little exercise that you can do for the next year. You can do it right now. You can wait until January 1st and start the New Year off this way. Or not, you can just start right now.

Make a list; I'm big on lists, a list of 100 goals to do in the next year 100 things to do in the next year.

Write today's date down and then of course that date one year from now. There's your starting point, there's your ending point.

Then just start writing. Start writing 100 things that you want to do. These don't have to be really big goals, "I want to start my own business. I want to become a movie star. I want to rule the world." Make them easy goals as well.

Just start writing some goals, things you've always wanted to do. "I've always wanted to go to Hawaii. I've always wanted to go sky diving. I've always wanted to try snorkeling. I've always wanted to take tap dancing lessons." Just start making a list.

Write all those things you've always wanted to do. Some people call this a bucket list, things you want to do before you kick the bucket, things you want to do before you die. Those are great but some of those things are huge things. They are things like; "I want to go to Egypt. I want to visit Russia. I want to see the Grand Canyon." Some of these things are huge, huge things that are going to take a lot of time, maybe even a lot of money to get done.

Now they are great goals to have, things you want to do before you die. But what about all those little tiny things that you've always kind of wanted to do but you didn't have time for them or they weren't a priority. Why not try to live your life with no regrets.

Make this list of 100 goals, 100 things to do this year. Make some of them big goals, make some of them little goals. Maybe one of the goals is, "Take my daughter out for ice cream once a week."

Maybe one of the goals is, "Tell my wife I love her at least 10 times a day." Maybe one of the goals is, "Tell my husband he looks good even though he doesn't."

Make them big goals. Make them little goals. Make them medium-size goals.

Just set some goals and then try and get as many as you can done before that year's up. See how many you can actually accomplish.

This is a great resource when you're sitting around going, "I'm bored. I got nothing to do." You could turn on the TV. You could surf around the internet and check your Facebook status for the 17th time today or you could go to your list of 100 goals and pick out one or two of them.

Maybe you can do it right now. Maybe you can start the process on some of them. Maybe you can get them done. Maybe you can get three or four done all at the same time.

What a great use of your time checking off some of these wonderful goals that you've set for yourself. So give it a try, set yourself 100 goals for the next year.

Remember your goals

Now if you're using some form of motivation to help you get your goal and I hope you are, one of the ways is your goal wall, putting your goal up there. And you have a reminder every day of what your goal is. It's right there in front of you all the time.

But even if you're doing that or if you're not doing it, sometimes these goals kind of go by the wayside. More important things come up. Life gets in the way, work, family, money, TV. Things get in the way and you forget about these goals.

I like to set up a series of emails to remind myself about the goals I've set especially if their big major goals, if they're long-term goals. "My goal is in the next 12 months to do this." Well it's probably not going to be top of mind every single day. So in order for me to not lose track I set up a series of email reminders.

There's a website called lettermelater.com. Also if you have a Gmail account there is an application called Boomerang. Basically what these two things do is they let you schedule emails to be sent out at a later date. Some email programs will do this already. Take a look at yours to see if it does it. If it does, use it.

What I'll do is I'll take my major goal and state it just like my goal statement on my goal wall, clearly defined, very specific. There's a deadline and I list some action steps that I will take to get this goal done and then I'll write down in big bold letters when that goal is going to be done, the deadline.

I'll setup a series of emails to be sent to myself once a week, once a month maybe. Maybe even a couple of times a week. It all depends on when your timeline of this goal is.

Now I'm getting updates all the time in my inbox, on my phone. Ping, "Hey don't forget about this goal of yours." A lot of times you won't even need to read the email. You'll look at it and be like, "What? I sent myself a...oh yeah, that's right, that goal of mine. I almost forgot about that. Thank goodness I set up this email reminder."

It just helps you to keep this goal top of mind. It helps so you won't forget about your goal and be one of those people New Year's Eve saying their resolutions for the year going; "Oh I forgot I was going to do that, wasn't I?" No, setup some email reminders and keep this goal top of mind.

Finally

There you have it; you've got your G.A.M.E. plan. Set a goal, take some action, motivate yourself, and evaluate to see if everything you're doing is working or not.

Discover your purpose behind your goal. Why do you want to have it accomplished? Why do you want to get this goal done?

Implement your passion. Make this goal of yours your passion. Make it something that you want, that you will get done.

Set a plan. Plan on success. Success doesn't just happen, plan on it.

Practice the skill sets that you need. Practice what you need to do to get this goal of yours completed.

Take a look at your mindset. Is resistance in your life? Is resistance keeping you from completing this goal of yours?

Are the people around you positive, encouraging people? Are they helping to motivate you?

Change the way you talk about your goal. No longer are you saying, "I want. I wish", but "I will. I have".

You, from this point on, will never fail again, will you? Because you are not failing, you're getting results. You're learning, you're learning what not to do. You're learning how to make this goal of yours happen.

All of this seems pretty simplistic when it gets right down to it. Making a list of ways to do something and then doing them. It's not rocket science, is it?

This is basic stuff that actually works, but its things that we weren't taught, things that we had to learn on our own, didn't we? There's no course in school on how to set a goal and get it completed. There should be.

Nobody ever taught us how to get what we want out of life. They just told us, "You can be anything that you want to be." They just forgot to tell us that we have to work really, really, really, really . . . did I mention really . . . really hard at it to get what we want.

No one's going to just give it to us. We have to work. We have to prepare. You know what; it's okay, because most people don't want to work that much to get what they want. You're different from that, aren't you?

You read this book. You bought this book. You've gotten this far in the book. Obviously, you are serious about your goals. You are serious about success. You are the kind of person that will get their goals done.

Think about it; a ship is safest when it's in the harbor, when it's docked in the harbor and sitting there. That is the safest it's ever going to be. Not much harm can come to that ship. Sure, there may be a storm coming in, but it's not as dangerous as it is out sailing the Seven Seas.

Guess what; that's not what a ship was made for. A ship was made to sail those Seven Seas; to go out, to transport people, to transport goods. It was made to sail, just like you.

You were not made to wallow in misery. You were not made to be just "good enough." You have ideas, you have goals, you have dreams, you have aspirations. You are, and you will go beyond "good enough."

I would love to hear about your successes, about your challenges, about your "failures" and about what you learned from them. Please, drop me a line,

fred@beyondgoodenough.com

I look forward to hearing from you and all the successes that you've accomplished.

Resources

Books worth reading

The Art of War
    By Steven Pressfield

Superpower
    By Ford Saeks

Awaken the Giant Within
    By Tony Robbins

Shut Up, Stop Whining & Get a Life
    By Larry Winget

See You At The Top
    By Zig Ziglar

The Magic of Thinking Big
    By David J Schwartz

The Power of Positive Thinking
    By Norman Vincent Peale

Poke The Box
    By Seth Godin

Please check out my weekly blog at:

www.BeyondGoodEnough.com

There I share a quick video with some insights into taking your business and your life...Beyond "Good Enough". Go figure!

I've also created an intensive video training course on how to get the results you want faster and easier than you ever though before.

www.10WeeksToResults.com

When something "bad" happens to you, there are 3 choices:

You can let it DEFINE who you are.
You can let it DEFEAT you.
You can let it DRIVE you.

Personally I'd go with #3 because the other two just plain suck.

-Fred Moore